Boxes

For a free color catalog describing Gareth Stevens' list of high-quality books, call 1-800-542-2595 (USA) or 1-800-461-9120 (Canada). Gareth Stevens' Fax: (414) 225-0377.

Library of Congress Cataloging-in-Publication Data

Griffiths, Rose.
    Boxes/ Rose Griffiths; photographs by Peter Millard.
      p. cm. — (First step math)
    Includes bibliographical references and index.
    ISBN 0-8368-1179-8
    1. Geometry—Juvenile literature. 2. Boxes—Juvenile literature. [1. Boxes.]
  I. Millard, Peter, ill. II. Title. III. Series.
  QA445.5.G75 1995
  516'.15—dc20   94-32472

This edition first published in 1995 by
Gareth Stevens Publishing
1555 North RiverCenter Drive, Suite 201
Milwaukee, Wisconsin 53212, USA

This edition © 1995 by Gareth Stevens, Inc. Original edition published in 1992 by A&C Black (Publishers) Ltd., 35 Bedford Row, London WC1R 4JH. © 1992 A&C Black (Publishers) Ltd. Additional end matter © 1995 by Gareth Stevens, Inc.

Series editor: Patricia Lantier-Sampon
Editorial assistants: Mary Dykstra, Diane Laska
Mathematics consultant: Mike Spooner

Illustration on page 27 by Terence Crump, The Cottage Studio.

Printed in the United States of America
1 2 3 4 5 6 7 8 9 99 98 97 96 95

First Step Math

Boxes

by Rose Griffiths
photographs by Peter Millard

Gareth Stevens Publishing
MILWAUKEE

What do you think is in my box?

中國福建烏龍茶
烏荈
净重125克

5

This box is almost the same shape as my wooden cube.

Which wooden block looks most like this box?

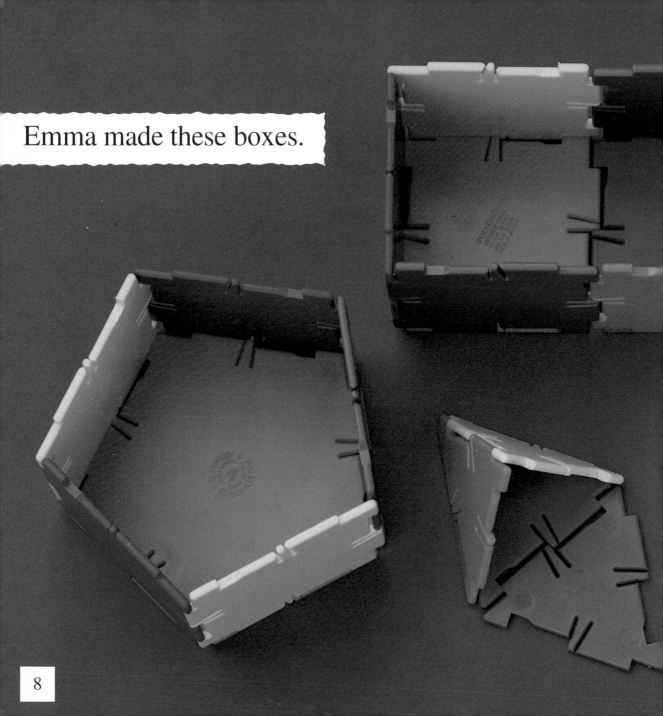

Emma made these boxes.

Each box is a different shape.

This box is bigger than me, and I can crawl inside it.

It's my playhouse.

10

This box is smaller than my hand.

Inside, there's a tiny hat shop.

These boxes fit
inside each other.

12

I can stack them on top of each other.

The smallest box is at the top.

The biggest box is at the bottom.

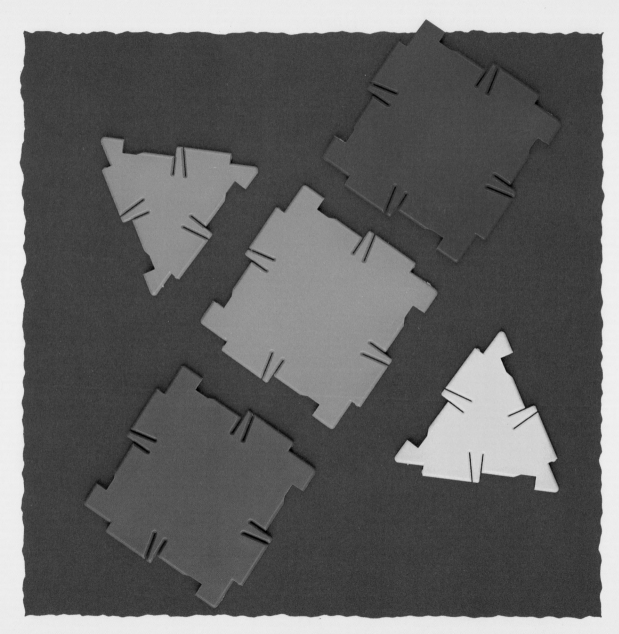

14 Tom is going to make a box with these pieces.

Tom's box holds eleven marbles.

I've filled my box
with popping corn.

I needed two and a half
big spoonfuls of corn.

16

How much corn
will I need to fill
this box?

17

I'm using a stencil to draw
a square on this cardboard.

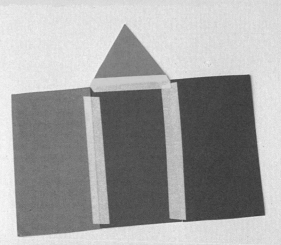

I've made these boxes without lids.

19

I've joined six squares of cardboard together with tape.

I can fold the squares up to make a box.

Will this fold up
to make a box?

Will this fold up
to make a box?

21

I'm making a box from one piece of cardboard.

The flaps help me
put the box together.

23

What shall we keep in our boxes?

I'm keeping treasure in my box.

FOR MORE INFORMATION

Notes for Parents and Teachers

As you share this book with young readers, these notes may help you explain the mathematical principles behind the different activities.

pages 4, 5, 24, 25
Sorting and classifying

Discuss ways of sorting boxes according to materials, size, shape, and purpose. Encourage children to look closely at both big and small boxes around them and to identify the different types.

pages 6, 7, 8, 9
Three-dimensional shapes

A cube is a three-dimensional shape that has six perfectly square faces (flat surfaces), or sides. Encourage children to experiment with combinations of shapes from a toy construction kit. See how many different three-dimensional shapes they can make.

Some children may want to name the geometric shapes they build. On page 8, one box is a pentagonal prism like the one below. Another is like a tetrahedron, made from four equilateral triangles. A shape made from twelve regular pentagons is a dodecahedron (see page 9).

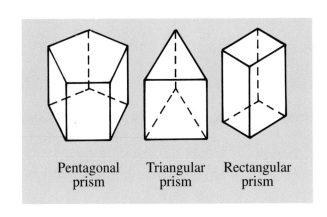

Pentagonal prism   Triangular prism   Rectangular prism

pages 10, 11, 12, 13
Comparing size and ordering
Before children can learn to measure objects successfully, they need considerable experience at comparing things directly and putting them in order according to size.

pages 14, 15, 16, 17
Measuring capacity
An object's capacity is the amount it will hold. Older children and adults may measure capacity in gallons, liters, or other standard measurements, but these are not appropriate for younger children. At first, use marbles, beads, or other uniformly sized objects that can be counted to see which box holds the most or least. Later, use spoonfuls of corn, dried peas, or sand.

Encourage children to estimate before they measure. Remember that the more quantities and objects they measure, the better they will estimate, so be sure to provide plenty of opportunities for them to practice.

pages 18, 19 Using stencils
Make or buy a set of stencils with a triangle, square, pentagon, and hexagon, all of which have sides of equal length, and a rectangle that has matching sides. When children experiment at making their own boxes, encourage them to draw, cut, and glue or tape as accurately as they can.

pages 20, 21, 22, 23 Patterns
Some six-square patterns can be cut in one piece and then folded into a box. Let the child decorate the unfolded box pattern and talk about what will happen when the box is folded up. For example, which sides will face each other?

Things to Do

1. Filling and measuring
Find some boxes of different shapes and sizes. Measure how much one of the boxes holds by filling it with spoonfuls of corn, beans, or dry cereal. Choose another box and guess first how many spoonfuls of corn it will hold, then check if you were right. Try again with some more boxes. Can you get better at estimating?

2. Nesting boxes
Make your own set of "nesting boxes" like Emma does on page 12 of this book by collecting small cardboard boxes of different sizes and similar shapes. Start with the largest box, then find the next largest and place it inside the first. Continue until all of the boxes have been "nested" inside the others. After making four or five nesting boxes, stack them on top of each other with the smallest box at the top and the largest box at the bottom, just like on page 13.

3. Finger puppet fun
Use empty matchboxes to make finger puppets. Cover each box with colored paper, then glue sequins, yarn, small buttons, or small bits of different-colored paper to make puppet faces or costumes. Leave one end of each box undecorated so you can later open and adjust the box to balance and move around on the tip of your finger. You can get ideas for decorating these puppets from fairy tale figures, favorite storybook and television characters, friends, or animal pals. You can even put on a play using your homemade box puppets.

Fun Facts about Boxes

1. Fabric-covered hatboxes were once commonly used to store and carry hats when traveling. Many hatboxes were round, although some could be different shapes.

2. Boxes are made from stone in many parts of the world. These small, decorative boxes are usually carved from a soft type of mineral called soapstone.

3. A box kite is made of two or more open-ended boxes that are connected by a wooden frame. The boxes of the kite have cloth sides stretched over the frame. Unlike other kites, box kites do not have tails.

4. In some countries, Boxing Day is celebrated as a legal holiday on December 26, the day after Christmas. On this holiday, people give presents in boxes to mail carriers, housekeepers, and tradespeople to thank them for their services.

5. In the early 1900s in America, people raised money for special causes by holding events called box socials. At the box social, lunches packed in boxes were auctioned off, or sold, to the highest bidders.

6. A box turtle is a type of land turtle that can pull its head and legs completely into its shell and then close up the shell with hinged joints. The turtle's body is then like a hard, sealed box, keeping it safe from predators.

Glossary

block — a solid piece of wood, metal, or some other material that has one or more flat sides.

crawl — to move slowly on hands and knees.

cube — a solid figure having six equal square sides that meet at right angles.

different — not like others; not the same.

flap — a flat piece attached along one side of a box or other object. A flap usually hangs loosely and is used as a cover for the object to which it is attached.

lid — a removable cover. Jars, plastic yogurt and margarine containers, and some boxes have lids.

pattern — a design; a model or plan for making something.

pieces — parts of a whole.

shape — the outer form of an object, such as an outline or tracing.

stack — to arrange objects into a pile or to put them one on top of the other.

stencil — a sheet of material, such as plastic or paper, out of which a letter or design has been cut. One stencil can usually be used over and over again.

treasure — something very valuable or precious.

Places to Visit

Everything we do involves some basic mathematical principles. Listed below are a few museums that offer a wide variety of mathematical information and experiences. You may also be able to locate other museums in your area. Just remember: you don't always have to visit a museum to experience the wonders of mathematics. Math is everywhere!

Museum of Science and Industry
57th Street and Lake Shore Drive
Chicago, IL 60637

The Smithsonian Institution
1000 Jefferson Drive SW
Washington, D.C. 20560

Royal Ontario Museum
100 Queen's Park
Toronto, Ontario M5S 2C6

San Francisco Craft and
Folk Art Museum
Building A, Fort Mason Center
San Francisco, CA 94123

Royal British Columbia Museum
675 Belleville Street
Victoria, British Columbia
V8V 1X4

More Books to Read

Action Contraptions
Mary and Dewey Blocksma
(Simon & Schuster)

Build It with Boxes
Joan Irvine
(Beech Tree)

Cups & Cans & Paper Plate Fans
  Phyllis and Noel Fiarotta
  (Sterling)

Fun with Paper
  Heather Amery
  (Reed International)

Things I Can Make
  Sabine Lohf
  (Chronicle Books)

When This Box Is Full
  Patricia Lillie
  (Greenwillow Press)

Videotape

My First Activity Video (Sony)

Index

blocks 7
boxes, capacity of
    15, 16, 17
boxes, shapes of 6, 9
boxes, sizes of 10,
    11, 12, 13

cardboard 18, 20, 22
crawling 10
cubes 6

drawing 18, 22

flaps 23
folding 20, 21

lids 19

making boxes 8, 14,
    19, 20, 21, 22, 23
marbles 15

patterns 22
playhouses 10
popping corn 16, 17

squares 18, 20
stacking boxes 13
stencils 18